MANNINGTREE STATION

Manningtree Station

A look at the railway station at Manningtree, Essex in 2007,
with reminiscences, photographs and history of former times.

By

David Cleveland

Manningtree Station 2007

Published by
David Cleveland
Manningtree
Essex
PO Box Manningtree 7608

2008
© David Cleveland

ISBN 978-0-9558271-0-5

British Library Cataloguing-in-Publication Data
A catalogue record for this book is available from the British library.

Designed by Ken Rickwood

Printed in Great Britain by PrintWright Ltd, Ipswich

Introduction

It was in 1969, when I moved to Manningtree, that I started to use Manningtree station to commute to London. I used to bicycle to the station with my eye on the tall semaphore signal that could be seen right down Station Road. If the signal was up I had to pedal faster. I had a couple of minutes at the most to get there, put my bicycle in the cycle shed, and jump on the train as it pulled into the station. The train got me to Liverpool Street at 8.37 am, then a half hour on the Central Line to White City, and I was at work.

After I left the BBC, I worked for a short time at the University of Essex in Wivenhoe Park - for which I travelled to Colchester by train - and kept another bicycle in the cycle shed there. Then for a year or two I deserted the railways and had a motor scooter.

In 1979 I changed job again, and started at the University of East Anglia, and began my journey by bicycle to Manningtree station to get the first train in the morning to Norwich, and the 7.00 pm back home in the evening. There were not many people travelling to Norwich at that time, and often I was the only passenger on platform 3, while opposite was crowded with commuters awaiting the London train, all looking at me wondering why I was going the other way. When my train came, I had a whole carriage to myself.

Throughout that time I occasionally took photographs of the station, the staff, and trains, for no good reason - except until now when I realise that they have become historic records. In 1979 I made a film showing the daily working of the station. It was shot mostly in one day, though some sequences were shot a few weeks later. It was at the time of further change at

Manningtree (mainly in readiness for electrification which did not come for a another six years) of lengthening the platforms at the Colchester end, doing away with local sidings, installing colour light signalling, and the de-commissioning of the signal box. I filmed the platforms and trains, the semaphore signalling system, and the shunting of trucks and wagons to the plastics factory siding. In the 1980s I made another film showing the electrification of the line between Colchester and Norwich. These films are on the DVD accompanying this book.

This book is just a personal record of what I have seen at the station, the people who worked there, the trains - in fact all the things that interested me as a local commuter, as well as hearing and reading about the history of Manningtree station.

Many people have helped me with information, and added to my collection of illustrations.

I would like to thank:- David Bramhill, Richard Brooks, Steve Brown, Danny Holland, Andy Kerridge, Ken Leighton, Bob Malster, Charles Marshall, Paul Osborne, David Owers, Russell Parker, Ken Rickwood, Michael Scurrell, Jamie Spurgeon and Barbara Westwood.

David Cleveland
August 2007

Contents

Front cover pictures: *Commuters waiting for an early morning train in the summer of 2007 and a BR station sign of the 1950s.*

Back cover picture: *The high trellis signal post from a 1978 water colour by Alan Drummond.*

Early morning commuters climb aboard the London train one sunny summer's morning in July 2007.

The Day Begins

It is 5.15 in the morning when the station staff at Manningtree come on duty. David Bramhill unlocks the entrance doors and fifteen minutes later Jamie Spurgeon gets ready in the ticket office. They only have a few minutes before the commuters arrive and the first of the busy commuter trains slides into platform 2 for London.

Hundreds of people line the platform to catch the nine up (that is, up to London) commuter trains that run during the first couple of hours. They are the 5.33, 6.03, 6.33, 6.43, 6.48, 7.03, 7.18, 7.25 and 7.33. These are fast trains to Liverpool Street, even though some stop at some intermediate stations such as Chelmsford and Stratford. All stop at Colchester, and one goes no further than Colchester - the 6.43 - for those that work in that town. Non stopping trains - that is at Manningtree - rush through, as do the occasional freight trains.

While the passengers are waiting, they have what perhaps is the most calming view of any station on this main Norwich to London line - green fields of rabbits, sheep, cattle, and the distant hills and trees of East Bergholt, Flatford and Dedham. On a summer's morning it is a delightful start to the day. On a cold winter's morning, it is night time.

The car park, with 500 spaces, soon fills up, and cars spread to the verges of the A137 to Cattawade. Cyclists and motor bikers arrive, their machines to be stored in the cycle shed or chained up outside on the newly created bike park.

A queue forms at the ticket office, particularly on a Monday morning when weekly tickets are purchased, but the happy smiling face of Jamie Spurgeon deals with it all calmly.

What with selling almost three hundred tickets, the 500 commuter cars, and those that arrive at Manningtree station by chauffeur driven cars (the wife), taxi, bus, cycle, or just plain walking, there must be a couple of thousand passengers using the station every day.

This is a far cry from when the railway opened in 1846 when the trains were few and far between. The first train to London started from Ipswich at 1.45 in the morning, calling at Manningtree at 2.15, and then virtually all stations to London, arriving in the metropolis at four minutes past five in the morning. This was classed as the morning mail train. Of course Liverpool Street as the London terminus did not exist in those days - the London station was called Shoreditch - later Bishopsgate in 1847. The opening of Liverpool Street to main line trains did not happen until 1875.

The next train to London from Manningtree was the 8.30 arriving in London at 11.0, followed throughout the day by the 10.30, 1.30, 4.0, and the last train of the day – at 5.30 pm. A copy of the Eastern Union timetable for June 1846 (the very first timetable) is reproduced in Hugh Moffat's "East Anglia's First Railways" published by Terence Dalton in 1987. In 1848, the six trains each way a day had increased to eight. Business must have been booming! That is what is recorded in William White's 1848 "History, Gazetteer, and Directory of Essex".

Manningtree station cycle park, July 2007.

The line is continually checked and maintained, particularly where the Harwich branch leaves the curving main line.

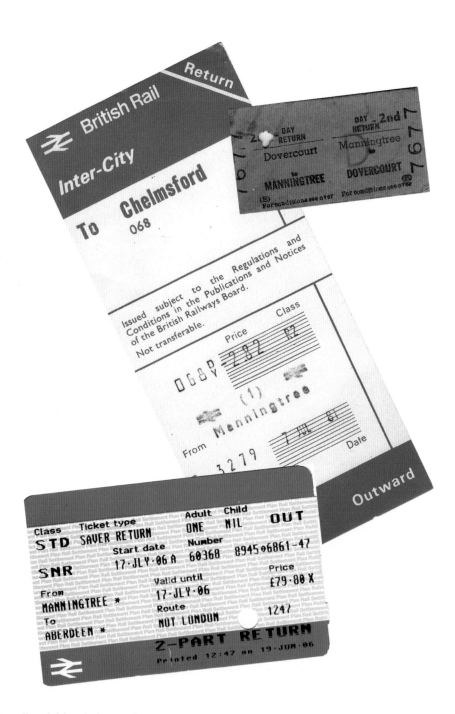

Old style cardboard ticket, the intermediate system of the 1970s and 80s, and the present credit card size ticket.

The view across the fields to Flatford and East Bergholt. July 2007.

A Country Station

Manningtree is the most countryfied station on the Norwich to London line. Nowhere else can passengers waiting for trains, or for that matter returning from hectic London, have a more peaceful view, of distant rolling countryside. Actually we are lucky to have the station at all, for the first scheme was for the line to run further to the west, with many brick arches to carry the track over the River Stour valley, the line running close to Flatford Mill.

Manningtree station is almost exactly half way between the two ends of the line, Norwich and London, and the journey is less than an hour to either place. In between are branch lines which can take you to Southend or Southminster, Braintree, Clacton, Frinton and Walton-on-Naze, Harwich and the continent, to Suffolk's towns and villages like Sudbury or Bury St

Edmunds and Newmarket, or along the East Suffolk line to Woodbridge, Saxmundham, Halesworth and Lowestoft. You can go to Yarmouth and the Norfolk Broads, to Cromer and Sheringham on the North Norfolk coast, to Cambridge, Ely and the Fens, or to Peterborough where connections can take you to virtually everywhere in the north and west of England, and all over Scotland. Manningtree is truly a magic place with endless destinations.

If you want to go to Norwich for the day, it will cost £15 off peak (2007 prices), if a jaunt to Harwich along the side of the Stour estuary is your pleasure, then it will cost you just £5. Of course if you get out at Harwich International you can book yourself on one of the ferries going to The Hook of Holland, or the delightful overnight trip to Esbjerg in Denmark.

If it is just London for the day then a Travelcard can be purchased for £44.10 before 9 o'clock, or £24.20 after. These tickets include travel on the underground and buses in London.

Commuters travelling every day to Liverpool Street have season tickets, which means they can travel on any train from 5.33 in the morning onwards. A Standard Class annual season ticket costs £3,960, or £6,320 First Class. All these prices of tickets were those current during the summer of 2007.

Many commuters can be seen scurrying to the Station Buffet to get a cup of tea or coffee to take on the train. The Station Buffet, which also opens early at 5.30 am, can supply you with a portable breakfast! For just £3 (2007 prices) you can get a box containing bacon, sausage, beans, hash brown, and scrambled egg - including disposable cutlery. I must try one of those.

The Station Buildings

The station buildings we see today are the result of a complete rebuild and layout at Manningtree between 1899 and 1901.

The main single storey building is in brick with stone window surrounds, with a main entrance with double doors to a small ticket-office area. By the entrance is an original Victorian red painted post box. There was until recently a small canopy on the outside of the main station building, over the entrance, but this has been removed.

The platforms, both on the up and down sides, had extensive awnings at one time to keep passengers dry. The awning stretched all along platform 2 to the subway, and similar on the down side. Around 1970 these were taken

Manningtree station forecourt - with a bus to Bildeston! July 2007.

Manningtree station before the last bit of awning on platform 3 was removed in 1979. Note the spikes on top of the station railings. These mysteriously disappeared about the year 2000 when they were sawn off.

The old stables. Now it is the office of Richard Tuck who is the agent for Italian manufacturers of clothing accessories. Mrs Tuck looks out on a bright summer's day in July 2007.

The Great Eastern style cycle shed photographed in 2007.

down leaving the awning we see on platform 2 today, and a short awning the length of the building on platform 3. This was removed in the late 1970s to allow, it is said, for electrical clearances when overhead power lines were to be put in place. It left the platform and its building, as well as passengers, as we can see today, drastically exposed.

In the late 1980s the main building on the up side was re-roofed. Unfortunately heavy tiles were used resulting in too much pressure on the walls, and in 1990 tie bars had to be inserted across the width of the building to prevent possible collapse. These can be seen as round metal discs on both sides of the building. Then the roof was stripped and new lighter tiles put on.

The building close to the main station on the south side is the former stable block. Horses at one time were used for moving trucks and wagons around in the yard, which is now the west car park.

According to Frederick Gant writing about his days in the early 1920s as one of two horse lads: "There were three horses doing duty at the station. One was fully employed on deliveries by van to Manningtree, the other two were for shunting. A perfect understanding existed between them and their handlers. They regularly worked on tracks next to the main lines, even as express trains thundered past. They were well cared for and made much of. All responded to names but also had numbers which were branded on the hooves of their fore-feet. The two horse lads worked overlapping shifts, helping as porters and working the level crossing gates. Very few vehicles had to cross the lines in those days, most were able to pass under the bridge on the road alongside".

Luckily the stables building is still intact, and adds to the shape and visual appearance of the station approach. Today it is the office of Richard Tuck who is the agent for Italian manufacturers of clothing accessories. Richard rents it from Network Rail.

Behind the stable, close to the up line, there were once cattle pens. These were used to hold livestock that had arrived by cattle truck, until the farmer could come and collect them and walk them away. Mrs Westwood, who lived in one of the cottages by the side of the level crossing approach, remembers cattle walking into their garden trampling on the flowers as they were driven on the hoof from the station to Lawford up Cox's Hill by local farmers.

In 1979 a rather plain box-type brick building close to the site of the old cattle pens, but on the present car park level, was put up to house electrical relay equipment.

Horse shunters posing for the camera at in 1922. The man on the left is William Durrant and on the right is Mr Harper.

There is one other small building that is worth mentioning, the cycle shed, an original Great Eastern building. The door to this faced the platform, so station staff could see who was using it at any time, and it was kept locked. When you wanted to put your bicycle in the shed, you went to the staff office where the key hung on a nail just inside the door. Known passengers would just open the office door and take the key, put their bicycle away, lock up and return the key. Less brave passengers knocked politely and asked for the key.

The shed therefore was a safe place to leave your bicycle. Station staff could easily see who went in and out of the shed as the entrance was visible from all platforms.

When the up platform was raised slightly in height, and lengthened at the Colchester end in 1978, the door was removed, the hole bricked up, and a new door put in on the south side. This unfortunately was not visible by staff, and thefts became common.

In the early 2000's the original wooden cycle racks inside the cycle shed were stripped out, and the interior is just a shadow of its former self – but outwardly it is still a good example of a Great Eastern Railway cycle shed. All these buildings belong to Network Rail, and are leased to, and operated by, the rail franchise holder, "One" Railway.

Not many cars about when this picture was taken in the 1970s. The level crossing gates are still in place.

Station Hotel and Other Buildings

The Station Hotel, now a privately owned building, still stands by the entrance road to Manningtree station. In the 1930s it is listed in Kelly's Directory as being run by Bertie Double. Today (2007) it is the registered office of CPd, "Perception in Design", a group of companies offering a range of services and products.

By the level crossing on the east side stood the Station Master's house. The last Station Master to live there was Tom Charlesworth, for in the 1960s the Area Manager from Colchester took over this role, and the house was demolished. Below this, in Station Road, by the junction, still stand four semi-detached houses put up in 1892 by the Great Eastern Railway for their staff. In 1966 British Rail decided to sell these houses, and the tenants were able to buy them on condition that they put in, at their own expense, mains water supply. Jim Westwood, a Senior Railman who had been at Manningtree since 1953, with his wife bought and lived in one of the houses.

Water & Water Tower

In the days of steam, sometimes locomotives needed to top up with water while standing at Manningtree. At both ends of platform 2, and at the Ipswich end of platform 3, there were cast iron columns with flexible leather pipes to feed the locomotive with water. The water came from the large tank on top of the water tower. Built in 1894, and situated behind the Station Hotel, this water tower was still standing in a dilapidated condition in 2007, though there are plans to remove it, so that the road can be widened.

There was, and still is, a pond close by to supply water. At one time there was a coal fired boiler and pump in the pumping house next to the water tower. This was manned round the clock. A small tunnel existed near the pond which went under the railway line to the field the other side. Michael Scurrell remembers as a child playing in this tunnel. It was filled in when the car park on the other side of Station Approach was constructed.

It was a common sight in steam days to see the locomotive bringing in the branch train from Harwich, run round, top up with water, and then join the carriages again. The cast iron columns gradually disappeared, but the one at the Colchester end of platform 2 remained until the 1970s before it was removed.

On the other side of Station Approach was a low lying area of land which often flooded, and helped supply water to the pond and water tower. This is now a car park.

Steam trains began to disappear quite early on this line. The first diesel locomotive to haul passenger trains ran in 1958, from then on diesel electric power soon took over from steam. The last steam train ran from Norwich in 1963.

Today trains have no difficulty charging up the slope to Ardleigh after leaving Manningtree station, but in the steam days it took a little longer to get up the two and a half mile incline of 1 in 134 between Manningtree and Ardleigh.

The water tower at Manningtree, standing unloved in 2007.

The cycle shed with its original door facing onto platform 2, and a redundant cast iron water column, still there in 1970.

Christine Cleveland and her children, Katharine, Elizabeth and Charlotte watch a train bound for London pass the hill just outside Manningtree station in 1982.

Published in June 1846, the illustration "shows the embankment crossing the two tidal and navigable forks or branches of the Stour, upon wooden viaducts intercepting a piece of land where the formation of a wharf and dock has been suggested". Note the slightly wider span with reinforcements on the left hand viaduct. Here was the deepest part of the channel used by river traffic, including sailing barges to Brantham Mill.

Beginnings

The line from London to Colchester was opened in stages by the Eastern Counties Railway Company, reaching Colchester in 1843. In July the following year work began by the Eastern Union Railway to reach Ipswich. Money was short, so the line had to follow the contours of the land, resulting in many curves. The line came close to Manningtree, though not exactly in the town, but the next best thing considering the obstacle of the Stour estuary. So Manningtree station is actually in the parish of Lawford.

Joseph Locke was the engineer, but in charge of the construction and the contractors was Peter Bruff. There were to be three stations, Ardleigh, Manningtree and Bentley, and the terminus at Ipswich beside Stoke Hill - now a housing estate built in 2007. The tunnel connecting to the line to Bury St. Edmunds (and Norwich) was not complete until November 1846.

There was a deep cutting to be made at Brantham with a lofty road bridge over it, and two wooden viaducts across the two channels of the River

Stour estuary. Between these two bridges there was to have been a quay for shipping, in fact there was a temporary wharf in use at the time when the bridges were constructed for the unloading of materials delivered by barge, but then the quay was never developed for commercial use.

These wooden bridges were replaced in 1904 with steel viaducts, which are still in use. Many of the original timbers of the wooden bridges were replaced in 1851, but some sawn off foundations can still be found at low water in the channel.

The line opened through Manningtree to Ipswich on 15th June 1846. On to Norwich took another three years, reaching there via Stowmarket and Diss in 1849.

According to Richard Brooks of Brooks of Mistley, the animal feed firm, one of his ancestors, William Brooks, who had granaries on Mistley Quay, owned the piece of marshland known as Hog Marsh between the two channels of the River Stour, and used it to graze cattle on. The cattle were ferried across the channel to the marsh - a laborious business. "When the railway company wanted to build the line across the marsh, he allowed them to do so with the right to drive cattle along the line for grazing - rather than ferry them by boat as he had no other access to the marsh".

The arrangement with the railway company gave William Brooks the right to drive cattle from the level crossing, across the south viaduct to Hog Marsh, with trains held until the line was clear. Whether this actually happened is not known, but apparently, according to Richard Brooks, the agreement allowed this.

Attfield Brooks, Richard's father, joined the Mistley family firm in the 1920s, and even then seemed to have extra powers over the railway. His son Richard records "My father exercised his right over the railway by staying at his desk in the office on The Walls until he heard the 9.11 am train to London go over the iron bridges and then drive to the station to get on the train. The station master always held the train for him! When my father retired he gave Hog Marsh and its rights to Essex Wildlife Trust".

The branch line from Manningtree to Harwich opened for business on 15th August 1854. At that time there was just the junction from the main line by the level crossing. The other connection, leading from the Harwich line by the Station Road bridge to the Ipswich line near the viaduct, was completed in

The north viaduct in the winter of 1991. Note the raised section on the left of the picture. This was over the deepest part of the channel allowing sailing barges and lighters to pass under the bridge.

The south viaduct over the River Stour during the severe winter of 1929.

A Diesel Multiple Unit on the Harwich branch line in August 1975. This photograph was taken close by the Station Road bridge. The area shown in the foreground is now covered with houses.

1882. This "north curve" as it was known was built at the same time as Parkeston Quay (now Harwich International) so enabling trains to travel direct to and from Ipswich and further afield. This direct route to and from Harwich and Ipswich served the cross country passenger trains from Harwich and the many goods and freight trains to and from the north using the port. Now our railway layout at Manningtree was complete.

It is supposed the railways immediately brought prosperity, and cheaper goods. Writing in poem form in 1855 about Manningtree in his "Reminiscences of Manningtree and Its Vicinity", Joseph Glass depicts another picture:

> *"But now, alas, the Eastern Counties Rail,*
> *Upsets the town and makes the business fail,*
> *And how to act our townsmen cannot tell,*
> *Some cottages will neither let, nor sell,*
> *All Manningtree, it seems, is out of course,*
> *And matters as they stand, can scarce be worse.*
> *But let us wait awhile, and we shall see,*
> *The future dawning of prosperity"*

Micaiah Aylward was buried in Lawford churchyard following his tragic death in 1874.

Early Days

Accidents and deaths on the railways were numerous during the early years of development and running. As early as 1864 a train from Harwich became derailed between Wrabness and Bradfield killing the stoker and injuring a number of passengers.

In Lawford Churchyard there is a gravestone reminding us of an accident at Manningtree ten years later, on 18th February 1874. A youth was employed at the station as "under horseman". His superior recounted at the inquest :- "On the afternoon of Wednesday, the 18th, about a quarter before two o'clock, the deceased and I fetched a horse box off the line of the Harwich branch to attach to the down train, and the deceased took the point to let the box cross the road. He went in front of the box, at the same time holding the chain attached to the horses and the box. When I got the distance required I called to the deceased to unlock the chain, and said 'all right'. I was at the time alongside the horses, and on turning round to see if the chain was unhooked, I saw the deceased in the act of falling, and as he was falling he called out 'oh', and immediately fell.

"The front wheel of the horse box passed over his shoulder, the horse box was thrown off the rails, and the hind wheel caught him in the back of the neck, upon which it rested. I immediately turned the horse round and drew it off, when he appeared quite dead. There was no horse in the box, but the box alone weighed five or six tons. The chain was not unhooked, and I should imagine that in attempting to unhook the chain, he missed his footing. He had been accustomed to this only for the last four months, but appeared quite up to it." The jury at the inquest recorded a verdict of "accidental death".

The unfortunate victim was Micaiah Aylward, the son of a Lawford labourer. He was buried on the railway side of the churchyard under some trees. The grave stone has since been moved, but is still accessible and visible.

This was not the only accident at Manningtree station. On the 8th December 1879, the three minutes past twelve from Ipswich non stop to Colchester passed through Manningtree at 12.18.

On the Colchester side of the station the line was being re-laid, and the gangs stood back as engine number 294 hurtled through. Three hundred yards later the engine shook and wobbled, and the wheels left the rails. The local paper reported "After proceeding some little distance tearing up the permanent way, and bending the rails like so much thin wire, the engine plunged down the embankment just short of the bridge that goes over the lane from Lawford Hall to the marshes, careered across the road, and did not stop until it had gone through the hedge into the field beyond. Some carriages remained on the railway embankment, others rolled down and got caught up in the trees. Farm workers and railwaymen ran to the scene and pulled out two injured people. One was the stoker, who died, the other a passenger, a Mr Page, a Long Stratton solicitor who had an injured knee". He had to be freed from the debris, and was then taken to the White Hart Hotel in Manningtree, given refreshment and put to bed, but soon recovered, and was able to ride out the next morning and inspect the scene of the accident".

A work train at Manningtree in August 1981. Railway enthusiast David Smith (with back to us) and his brother Jonathan, joined by Elizabeth and Charlotte Cleveland.

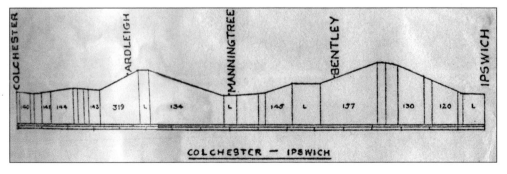

Colchester - Ipswich gradients. L indicates level. The climb from Manningtree to Ardleigh indicated as 134 means that the track rises by 1 foot in every 134 feet.

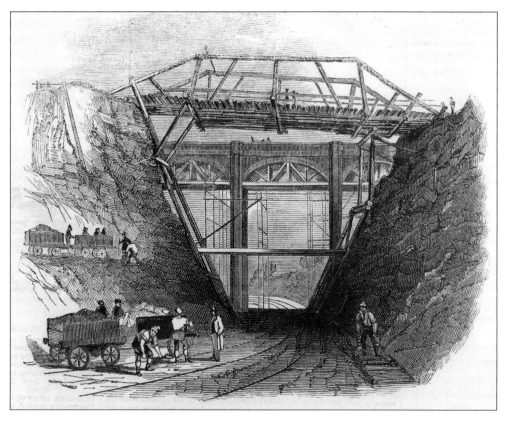

Brantham bridge and cutting under construction in 1846.

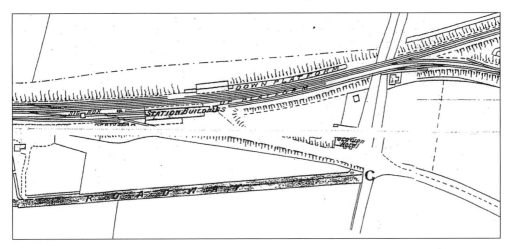

The layout of the station before the 1899-1901 alterations.

Victorian Alterations

Between 1899 and 1901 there were considerable alterations to both the layout of the lines and the station buildings. A complicated "Indenture made the twenty fifth day of January 1899…." gave the Great Eastern Railway access over the track owned by the Lawford Hall Estate (marked roadway on the map) which runs the other side of the present car park in front of the station. This was so the railway could get road vehicles to and from their proposed new goods yard situated where today the west car park is.

In return the railway was "to keep in perpetuity the same roadway between the said points B and C in a good and proper state of repair and condition". The present short road by the stables connecting the west car park with the station forecourt did not exist at that time.

However, there was a footpath shown from the station buildings leading to the "roadway". Today this footpath is not much in evidence - it is between the two car parks - but there was a time when it was properly kept, with a gate and fencing between the railway property and the road. There are two public footpaths on this "roadway" opposite the station, one goes straight ahead up the hill to Lawford Church, and the other follows the railway line to the west, turns right under the railway bridge (you cannot turn left as this is a private road to the farm) and continues to the south channel of the river Stour. Here you can go right to Cattawade, or left to Flatford Mill and Constable Country.

The "indenture" of January 1899 also included a map of the track layout as it was, and it is interesting to note that there was no loop line round the back of the down platform, no goods yard with tracks in it, and that the signal box was the Colchester side of the station by some sidings.

The original station buildings, probably wooden structures, were demolished, and the new main building on the up line and the shorter building on the down line built, along with the stables, and according to Peter Kay in his "Essex Railway Heritage" published in 2006, the building in the goods yard as well - demolished in the 1970s to make the new west car park. These buildings were designed by William Ashbee, the Great Eastern Railway architect. At the same time alterations were made to the track layout of the station, and all this work took until 1901. This was a time of booming business, with faster trains than ever before, principally due to better designed steam locomotives.

The curved cast iron spandrils which help support the beams of the station canopy.

The caption on this photograph reads "The Royal Train returning from Norwich. Taken near Manningtree".
It is thought to be 1909. It is seen here crossing the south viaduct heading towards London.

Edwardian Adventures

Perhaps the most famous story revolving around Manningtree station was that of the escaped nun from the East Bergholt Benedictine Convent in 1909.

Margaret Moult entered the convent in 1902 at the age of seventeen, and had a very difficult time there over a seven year period.

From an early age Margaret Moult was attracted by the "beauty and holiness of the life of a nun". At East Bergholt the daily routine was demanding. Up at 5.00 am, followed by three hours in church before breakfast at 8.00 am, bread and butter and a mug of tea or coffee - consumed standing up. At 8.45 am the nuns went to carry out their various occupations of the day, such as book binding, printing, church embroidery, making clothes etc.

which brought in money to the Convent, as well as helping keep the place in good habitable order by doing such jobs as painting, paper hanging, carpentry, cooking, washing, ironing, gardening etc.

At 11.30 am readings from the bible, followed by dinner in the refectory. The food, normally a small amount of meat or dried fish, was eaten in silence. Needlework followed for an hour when they could talk to each other but "must not hold private conversations or speak on worldly subjects". At 1.15 pm "devotions in the church". At 3.00 pm "the nuns work together in silence at whatever the Abbess has appointed". 4.00 - 4.30 spiritual reading, 4.30 - 5.00 meditation in church, with supper at 6.00 pm. "The food at this meal is usually milk pudding, porridge, pastry or vegetables" After three quarters of an hour in the work room, there was singing in the church, followed at 8.30 pm by ninety minutes of prayer and meditation. Then each nun went to her cell, furnished with one "small straw bed", a small table and chair, and "a crucifix and a few holy pictures". Baths were not permitted, and washing and cleaning of teeth (one tooth brush supplied new each year) had to be done using a small can of hot water in the cell before lights were put out.

Writing in 1909 after she had escaped, Margaret Moult says "A young girl is expected to follow the wretched, dreary routine …. to pray, and meditate all day through, to live a life of absolute loneliness, without so much as a single friend - yet Christ in his mortal life had friends; to exist on the barest necessities of life; and behold, it is a grievous crime, a mortal sin capable of casting the soul headlong into hell, to so much as desire anything beyond".

On top of this was the dreadful food, the absence of medical care, the strict rules and whims of the Abbess, which if broken resulted in some form of penance such as lying prostrate on the floor, or carrying out physical tasks sometimes for weeks, and the whispering, spying and reporting fellow nuns, the back biting, spitefulness, and the "jealousy and meanness".

Eventually, after seven long years, Margaret Moult began to have "regrets for the course I had taken". It all became too much, and in 1909, she escaped. The story is told in a very moving book Margaret Moult wrote almost as soon as she got out - "The Escaped Nun" published by Cassell and Company.

On the night of Monday 15th February 1909, Margaret Moult managed to get out of the convent. The night was dark, and having been inside for seven years, she was not sure which way to go to get to the station - for her intention was to get a train to London where her mother lived.

The Station Hotel in 1911. It must have been built about the time the line opened, as it is recorded as being there in 1848. It remained a pub until about 1973. The road to the station can be seen in this photograph, with the fence on the left hand side which Margaret Moult clung to when being physically persuaded (unsuccessfully) to return to the convent.

After half running, half walking, and stumbling into ditches, and asking strangers the way, she managed to get to the bottom of Station Approach by the Station Hotel. There a horse drawn waggonette drew up, and out jumped the gardener and two Sisters. Margaret ran across to the other side of the road, and held onto the wooden fence while the sisters grabbed her and tried to pull her away. Her screams were heard by station staff, and two porters, Frederick Munnings and Levi Rumsey, came down to see what was happening. The Sisters stood back. It was raining hard, and Margaret persuaded the group to shelter under the canopy of the station entrance. There they met Foreman Porter John Disbrey. Arguments followed with the Sisters, with dire warnings of what awaited Margaret in the next world, when the station master, Frederick Swann, came out to see what the commotion was about.

The Sisters pointed out she had no money for the train. Margaret replied "My mother will pay at the other end". They said she could not stay at the station. "Then I shall stay in the road" said Margaret. Mr Swann listened to all this, summed up the situation, and said "If you make it quite clear to the lady Abbess, in what spirit I assist this young lady, merely to avoid scandal for the Abbey, I will lend her the money to go to her friends in London". Mr Swann lent her "half a sovereign" – five shillings for the train fare, and five shillings for a cab at Liverpool Street to her mother's home.

Mr Swann put her in the waiting room where there was a warm fire. He even "ordered me some refreshments, the first I had eaten that day". It was 8.30, and the next train, the mail train, was not due until 1.20 in the early hours. "The hours seemed to pass away very slowly, but I was unable to sleep, for I still expected to see some of the nuns again".

The train eventually came, and she was put into a compartment next to the guard. She was the only passenger as the train pulled out of Manningtree station. "It was with the utmost satisfaction that I leaned back in the carriage, knowing myself to be each moment going father away from East Bergholt"

Margaret Moult.

Margaret Moult's story made the papers, and she became headline news. The Protestant Alliance gave a gold watch each to the station master and the porters, together with a bible and "Foxe's Book of Martyrs". Mr Tom Sloan, an MP, interviewed Margaret Moult to obtain evidence for his bill for the inspection of conventual and monastic institutions, and the "Escaped Nun" herself travelled widely on a speaking tour, lecturing on convent life and its dangers. Her book went into a second enlarged edition in 1911, by which time she was married. Manningtree station plays a by no means small part in this fascinating and moving true story.

On Thursday 17ᵗʰ June 1909 Margaret Moult returned to Manningtree and met the staff of Manningtree station. From left to right, the man in the peaked cap is one of the porters who helped the "escaped nun", Frederick Munnings. Next to the lady holding an umbrella is Frederick Swann, the station master in his braided peaked cap. Margaret Moult stands behind the little boy, with her mother on her left. On the right of the picture stands foreman porter John Disbrey and at the very edge of the photograph, porter Levi Rumsey.

Manningtree station, platform 2 in 1911.

A Giraffe

The Edwardian period was a time of further expansion and fast trains - some of them rushing non stop through Manningtree, in fact not stopping anywhere. There was the Norfolk Coast Express to Cromer (Liverpool Street 1.30, Cromer arrival 4.25)– non stop from Liverpool Street to first stop North Walsham (a distance of 130 miles) then on to Cromer; a similar non stop train to Yarmouth in two and a half hours; and of course the boat train to Harwich direct from Liverpool Street - which in 1904 was equipped with corridor carriages and a restaurant car.

It is hard to imagine now the amount of goods, fruit, vegetables, fish, coal, grain, flour, cattle cake, etc, and objects large and small which were carried by the railways. An idea can be drawn of the amount of traffic when one considers the fact that there were a million trucks on British railways in the middle of the last century, many being owned by the railway, others privately owned. Many of these would be carrying coal, for which every station had a siding. Operated by commercial organisations, in East Anglia most stations had the sign "Moy" indicating that this family firm had a coal depot at the station. Though the chief office of Thomas Moy was in Colchester, and they had a depot at Ardleigh, they did not have one at Manningtree, for all coal was distributed in the Lawford, Mistley and Manningtree area by local merchants – Charles Stone and Son of Norman Road, Mistley; Smith Bros. of Station Road; Miller and Son, Bradfield; Large and Sons, Bradfield; and Charles Catling of Bradfield. Most coal seemed to have been distributed from neighbouring Mistley station, on the Harwich branch line.

Manningtree station itself had coal fires until the late 1970s, with the coal being regularly delivered by rail for consumption in offices, waiting rooms and the signal box.

For all this work, large numbers of staff were required. An example of the number of people who worked at Manningtree station can be observed by the report of the annual dinner held at the White Hart public house in Manningtree on 7th February 1913, when over fifty people attended. "Mr Swann, the Station master presided over a company numbering nearly sixty. The usual toasts were honoured, and songs, and other items were contributed. The arrangements were efficiently carried out by a committee consisting of

Messrs P. H. Turner, E. Ainger, W. Punchard and Ridgeon" according to the "Great Eastern Railway Magazine".

Livestock was carried from most stations at one time, and there were special cattle trucks for livestock, including horses, and even occasionally performing animals for the circuses which visited local towns. Even the guards van might have live animals in it such as pigeons on their way for release in some far distant corner of the country.

In fact, these birds were still being carried as late as the 1970s. In 1979 there was a poster at Manningtree station stating that "on and from 29 April 1979 unaccompanied livestock cannot be accepted at this station".

Perhaps the weirdest freight - if that is the word - to be seen passing through Manningtree must have been a giraffe in 1909 on it its way to Ipswich. Don't worry - it was stuffed. According to the "Great Eastern Railway Magazine": "Had this creature remained as pliable when inanimate as when animate, there would have been no difficulty; but stuffed, mounted and wrapped in canvas, it could neither bend its haughty neck nor even turn down its stiffened ears in order to facilitate conveyance by rail, hence all the trouble that followed. First came the knowledge that even when loaded to the best advantage on the lowest available truck, its ears would exceed the gauge limits".

The report goes on "The Company's engineer was consulted and gave his certificate, with the proviso that an inspector should travel with the load and take extreme care in going dead slow under a certain bridge. Arrangements were made accordingly, a suitable low road float brought the giraffe to the station, and after a lengthy process of transferring from float to truck, properly adjusting thereon, sheeting and roping and testing under two gauges, lo and behold the whole load, including the sheets and ropes, cleared the gauge by about an inch. This was of course an agreeable surprise, but to guard against possibilities, the inspector was instructed to see the load through and the suggestion made that he should travel jockey fashion on the animals neck. The inspector, however, successfully pleaded age, weight and non-training, against that method, and was therefore allowed to enjoy the usual need of comfort obtainable in the brake of a goods train"

The 16 foot 10 inch high giraffe (the lowest bridge was 13 foot) was wrapped up so no one realised what went through Manningtree station. What a shame. The stuffed giraffe is still on display in Ipswich Museum, which it made safely, and is labelled "lent by John Hall of Broughton". Let's hope he does not want it back.

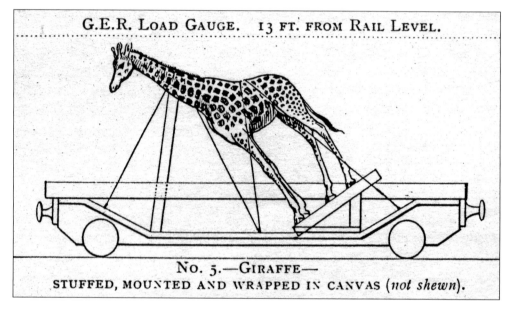

G.E.R. LOAD GAUGE.   13 FT. FROM RAIL LEVEL.

NO. 5.—GIRAFFE—
STUFFED, MOUNTED AND WRAPPED IN CANVAS (*not shewn*).

The stuffed giraffe which travelled through Manningtree on its way from London to Ipswich in 1909.

Manningtree station staff in 1922.

Porter	Horse Shunter	Horse Lad	Horse Lad	Shunter	Station Foreman	Porter	Porter Lampman	Signalman	Shunter	Horse Shunter	Station Foreman
-----	E.Redgrave	W.Durrant	F.Gant	B.Finney	Chambers	R.Edwards	-----	-----	W.Piper	Mothersole	J.Disbery

Ticket Collector	Clerk	Booking Clerk	Station Master	Goods Clerk	Clerk	Booking Clerk
-----	-----	French	Leverett	Turner	-----	-----

Refreshment Room Lad in front

The Station in 1922

A photograph of Manningtree station staff in 1922 shows 20 people lined up before the camera. According to Frederick Gant, who joined the staff in 1918, and worked there until 1925 as a lad looking after horses (he can be seen fourth from the left on the back row), there were four or five other staff not included in the photograph - presumably because they were running the station or on another shift at the time. This makes a total staff of somewhere around 25 people.

The station master at this time was Mr Leverett who wore a frock coat with gold coloured insignia. He lived in the station master's house by the side of the level crossing.

Frederick Gant's memories go on: "On day shift duties were two booking clerks, two clerks in the parcels and telegraph office, a ticket collector, a station foreman, a shunter, two horse shunters, and two horse lads, a goods clerk, a goods yard foreman, and a porter.

"There were three young ladies running the two station refreshment rooms, one on the up platform, the other on the down line, with a lad to assist them. This lad had also to walk the length of all passenger trains carrying quite a heavy basket tray supported in front of him by a wide strap around his shoulders, containing sweets, chocolates, cakes, etc. for sale. He is the one seated in front on the photograph, wearing a smart uniform with gold coloured piping.

"One of the day duty porters also acted as lamp man, and was responsible for all the signalling lamps, level crossing gates lamps etc. This was quite a responsible job, and an arduous one, especially on the exposed stretch of line by the bridges where he had also to do duty as a fog signaller without any shelter or protection from the weather.

"There was also an elderly widow who walked from Dedham one or two days a week to scrub the floors of offices and the waiting rooms".

The station was, in 1922, very much like it is today, except for more staff, and considerable activity with goods, mail bags, luggage etc.

"There were three waiting rooms on the up - a 1st class, 3rd class, and a ladies, and the same on the down line platform. All were provided with coal fires".

Mr Gant remembers a dozen or so "penny in the slot" machines placed around the platforms dispensing confectionery, mostly bars of chocolate. There was also a W. H. Smith & Sons book stall situated by the booking hall doorway on platform 2. There were about twenty barrows with iron wheels for the station staff to use for passengers' luggage and the wide variety of goods handled at the station.

At 10 o'clock every morning a whistle was blown so that all clocks and watches could be synchronised.

In the old goods yard, now the car park the Colchester side of the station, there were at one time roughly made wooden huts (made out of railway sleepers) for the gang of platelayers. The men, according to Frederick Gant recalling the way of life in the early 1920s, wore "corduroy trousers with leather straps below their knees, these gave more freedom of movement and also lessened wear and tear at the knees of the trousers. Trousers worn in this manner were called lijahs". This is an old Suffolk term used by farm workers.

"At times the plate layers used a four wheeled trolley on the tracks when moving heavy materials. When laden they propelled it by using long flat wooden levers with holes in the ends. These fitted over metal pins projecting from the wheels near the rims. They had "T" shaped handles at the other ends. Four men would stand on the platform of the trolley above the wheels, two on one side would push down with the levers they were holding when the pins were at the top of the wheels. At the same time the two men on the other side would pull upwards as the pins on the wheels on their side would be at the bottom and so they sailed along by continuous pump like pushing down and pulling up movements".

When travelling down gradients the levers were used for braking by inserting them between the sides of the trolley and the insides of the rims or flanges of the wheels.

When it was necessary to clear the track, the trolley had to be lifted off by hand. When not in use it was secured by lock and chain and the key kept by the foreman platelayer. The stretch of line for which each gang of platelayers were responsible was called "the length". On some of the bigger track repairs there would be a look out man. He wore a brassard, carried a green and a red flag, and sounded a raucous note on a trumpet to give warning of approaching trains.

Frederick Gant remembers five signal boxes when he was there in the early 1920s.

"The station and junctions were controlled by five signal boxes. One within a short distance of each end of the station. Another at what was then the Xylonite factory at Brantham where there was also a siding, and one at each end of the loop line. The latter two were manned by two eight-hour shift signalmen and closed at night when the loop line was not in use. Signalling was then switched through to the other signal boxes".

In 1924 three of the signal boxes were decommissioned. The box on the Colchester side of platform 2 went, as did the two boxes on the north curve or the loop line as Mr. Gant calls it. The signal box by the level crossing was enlarged and track circuiting installed - so the signalmen could see where trains were at any one time. The plastic factory siding box which Mr Gant recalls must also have gone at this time.

000	London(Liverpool Street).
$1\frac{1}{4}$	Bethnal Green.
$2\frac{1}{4}$	Coborn Road.
4	Stratford.
$4\frac{1}{2}$	Maryland Point.
$5\frac{1}{4}$	Forest Gate.
$6\frac{1}{4}$	Manor Park.
$7\frac{1}{4}$	Ilford.
$8\frac{1}{2}$	Seven Kings.
$9\frac{1}{4}$	Goodmayes.
10	Chadwell Heath.
$12\frac{1}{2}$	Romford.
$13\frac{1}{2}$	Gidea Park & Squirrels' Heath.
15	Harold Wood.
$18\frac{1}{4}$	Brentwood & Warley.
$20\frac{1}{4}$	Shenfield & Hutton.
$23\frac{3}{4}$	Ingatestone.
$29\frac{3}{4}$	Chelmsford.
36	Hatfield Peverel.
$38\frac{3}{4}$	Witham.
$42\frac{1}{4}$	Kelvedon.
$46\frac{3}{4}$	Mark's Tey.
$51\frac{3}{4}$	Colchester.
56	Ardleigh.
$59\frac{1}{2}$	Manningtree.
$63\frac{1}{4}$	Bentley.
$68\frac{3}{4}$	Ipswich.
$71\frac{1}{4}$	Bramford.
$73\frac{1}{2}$	Claydon.
$77\frac{1}{2}$	Needham.
$80\frac{3}{4}$	Stowmarket.
83	Haughley.
$86\frac{1}{2}$	Finningham.
$91\frac{1}{2}$	Mellis.
95	Diss.
$97\frac{1}{2}$	Burston.
$100\frac{1}{2}$	Tivetshall.
104	Forncett.
$106\frac{3}{4}$	Flordon.
$109\frac{3}{4}$	Swainsthorpe.
114	Trowse.
115	Norwich(Thorpe).

There were 40 stations between Liverpool Street and Norwich in 1922.

There were signal boxes at one time on each apex of the triangle. Here is clearly seen the box on the Harwich branch line by the bridge in Station Road. This is from a postcard of 1907.

The boat train - The Flushing Continental - direct from Liverpool Street to Parkeston Quay on the Harwich branch line. The photographer is standing just about on the Station Road bridge. The north curve going round to meet the main line to Ipswich can be seen on the right.

45

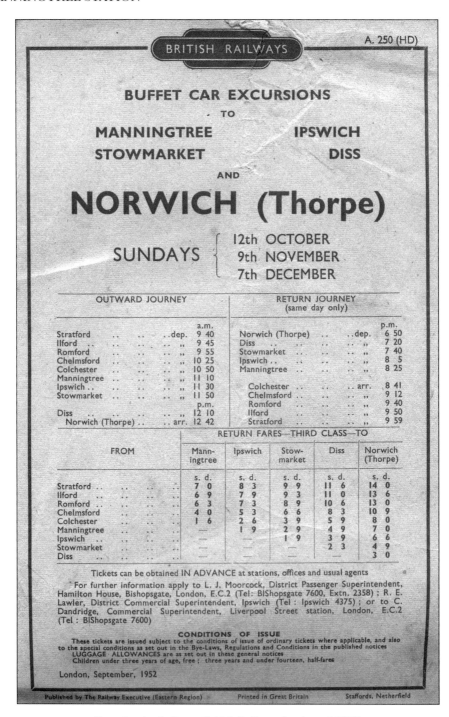

Excursion details from a British Railways handout of 1952.

"The East Anglian" an express service of 2 hours 10 minutes between Norwich and Liverpool Street in the late 1950s.

The 1940s and 50s

1939-45 War

Manningtree, like all stations in the war, was busy with extra trains. These were trains carrying munitions, troops, military and naval equipment, tanks, coal and fuel, and all the extra things required at short notice for a country at war.

In 1939 evacuees from London were transported to Ipswich, Clacton, Walton, Felixstowe and Woodbridge. A year later, with the threat of invasion, it was decided that these evacuees, along with local children, should be moved again, as they lived too near the coast. Twenty-three trains were scheduled to move over 11,000 people to South Wales.

Then there were trains carrying rubble from bombed London for use as foundations for runways for the new airfields in East Anglia, along with bricks, tarmac, steel and cement. There were "leave" trains for the British army travelling from Harwich and Parkeston to London, and special forces postal trains.

On the East Coast there were a few armoured trains - in 1941 Charles Bayes was travelling from Liverpool Street to Yarmouth when he noticed an armoured train with a "gobbler" on the front standing at Manningtree. A gobbler was the old nickname for a particular type of tank locomotive which consumed large amounts of coal.

In 1940, with the worries of possible invasion, to prevent trains falling into enemy hands it was decided that no locomotives should be left overnight at stations by the coast. At Harwich therefore, all engines were moved to Manningtree for the night. Luckily Manningtree at this time had plenty of sidings around the station and in the goods yard to accommodate these locomotives. On top of all this, men had to work in the dark around the station and tracks as no lights were permitted.

According to ganger E. W. Stannard of Manningtree, recorded in "By Rail To Victory" by Norman Crump in 1947, as an anti invasion precaution, the piers of the viaducts over the Stour at Manningtree were mined with charges inserted. One day a wagon on a train standing by the viaduct caught fire. Mr Stannard happened to be close by, and without thinking of the danger of the mined bridge and the fire, went up and down the embankment getting buckets of water to put the fire out. After about twenty minutes he extinguished the fire. For this heroic action, he received the B. E. M. and L. N. E. R. medals.

The railings along the side of the road up to the station somehow survived the war, but the railings outside the railway workers' cottages were taken away along with many other people's iron work towards the war effort. The remaining station railings mysteriously had their sharp top points sawn off around the year 2000, presumably in case someone became impaled and sued the railways.

The tracks took a pounding during the war and it took many years to renew the rails in the 1940s to get the railway system into good condition again.

1953 Flood. This photograph taken the day after from the signal box looking towards Cattawade shows the flooded fields, the A 137, and the approach to the level crossing on the left hand side.

1953 Flood

The severe flooding that occurred on the night of 31ˢᵗ January 1953, which affected the East Coast from the Wash to Canvey Island, breached the sea walls at Manningtree. It spread almost to the station itself. The salt water flooded in across the fields where the industrial estate now is, under the railway bridge and up Station Road as far as the Station Hotel. It also came from the Cattawade road side and into the underpass. In fact it probably went a little way up the station approach, as the water came up to the window sills of the railway workers' cottages, making the water several feet deep at the cross roads.

Mail Train

It was a common sight, before the Post Office decided to send the mail by road, to see mail bags being loaded into the guards van of passenger trains. There was one passenger train, the 7.0 pm from Norwich, which had a Travelling Post Office attached to it just behind the locomotive. At one time the non stopping Travelling Post Office (TPO) collected the mail at high speed from a device beside the line close to the Flatford footpath bridge.

The postman in his GPO mail van travelled up the private road track about 7.50 pm, and made his way up the steps of the embankment. Here, on the up line was a post with an arm on it. The leather pouch of mail was hung on the end of the arm, which was then swung out so as to be close to the passing train. The non stopping train had a hinged apparatus with a net on the side of the TPO carriage. As the net caught the bag from the post, it thudded down into the carriage by the feet of the waiting TPO men. This happened extremely fast, and you had to keep your distance, but at least the mail was on its way to London. This method ceased at the end of the 1950s, but the net apparatus was still to be seen on the side of the TPO van until the 1970s, but by that time the train stopped at Manningtree station - though even that ceased in May 1990 when TPO's were withdrawn. This was the only TPO to be attached to a passenger train on a scheduled service. The service had its origins as far back as 1868 when a special sorting tender ran from Ipswich to London. Incidentally on the side of the train was a posting box, so any person rushing to get a letter to London could actually post it as the train stood in the station.

A Victorian illustration of a mail pouch being picked up by a fast moving Travelling Post Office (TPO) van.

A Norwich bound train in the Queens Jubilee year livery of 1977.

The 1960s and 70s

Russell Parker started work at Manningtree station in 1963, and remembers the number of staff there at the time. "There were four porters, two booking clerks, one goods clerk, three shunters, and three foreman. There was Jack Fuller working in the goods yard, where a Scammell three-wheel road vehicle came from St Botolphs station to deliver parcels. Then there was the gang in the hut looking after the permanent way, fences and mowed the banks. Just before then there were also signal fitters, Bert Howes and Jim Edwards, who oiled the signal wires and dealt with points failures, and Bill Lister who dealt with telephones and track circuits".

Some timetables included exact distances. For instance the mileage from Manningtree to Liverpool Street was listed as fifty nine and a half miles.

The 1964 timetable lists six through trains to London in the morning (7.22, 7.42, 8.22, 8.58, 9.35, 11.35) and six in the afternoon / evening (1.35, 3.35, 5.35, 6.58, 9.03, 9.58). Many of these took about an hour and fifteen minutes to reach Liverpool Street - some even longer. The fare listed is 1st class 22/6 (£1.12p) and 2nd class 15/- (75p).

The 1972 timetable lists fewer trains than we are used to today. The morning rush consisted of the 7.22, 7.48, 8.21, and 8.59 to London Liverpool Street, the quickest of these taking just over an hour and five minutes. There were a couple of earlier trains at 6.24 and 6.59 for commuters to Colchester only, where passengers could change for London arriving at 7.45 and 8.27. During the day the service was one train every two hours.

An "up" train coming into Manningtree in the 1970s. Note the old track layout and the signal box close to the level crossing.

When there was just a two hourly service for both the up and down main lines, the Norwich to London trains often arrived at the same time as the London to Norwich.

Platform 1, the bay for the branch line connection, photographed in August 1979. Here is one of the diesel multiple units, which disappeared from the Harwich branch when electrification came.

The junction at the bottom of Station Approach before the roundabout and housing estate were built. Photograph taken in July 1979.

March, 1978. Work begins (though no one working in this picture) lengthening platform 3. Note the high trellis signal post on the extreme left of this photograph.

The new track layout being worked on in 1979. The signal box is still working the semaphore signals, and the gates are still in place across the level crossing. The new colour light signals are being installed ready for the switch over. This one is at the end of platform 1 for the branch to Harwich.

Further changes to cope with increased traffic, longer trains, and the proposed electrification of the line were made at Manningtree in the 1970s and early 1980s. This work of course happened at many other stations along the line at the same time.

Around the back of the buildings on platform 3 runs a siding. This was connected at the Colchester end to the main down line at one time, and thus formed a loop. This was disconnected leaving just a single siding. This has been used for the odd engineering machine to park overnight.

The remaining awning on platform 3 was removed, and small brick buildings over the subway were constructed, with a little seat inside - though unprotected from driving rain.

In the old goods yard area, a new brick electrical relay building was put up in 1979. The platforms at the Colchester end were lengthened, and at the

Ipswich end, the platforms altered - particularly the up. This was shortened to make better access for the branch line trains to platform 1, and to allow a new track layout at the junction with the Harwich branch.

At this time the Manningtree signal box, situated close to the level crossing, was manned around the clock by three signalmen working shifts - Danny Holland, John Donnelly and John Crane. During daylight hours there was an additional box lad working from 6.40 am to 2.00 pm then another lad working from 2.00 pm to 9.40 pm. When there were two on duty in the box, one would open and close the level crossing gates – normally the lad. When only one was on duty, then one of the station staff would deal with the gates.

Rail traffic flowed through Manningtree in the night, and there were trains that stopped and had to be dealt with. There was the paper train that left Liverpool Street at around 2.40 am, arriving at Manningtree at approximately 3.50 am. The papers had to be "barrowed" across the Colchester end line crossing, and then collected from the station by the paper shops. Then there was the 3.00 am coal truck train from Ipswich, which had to be shunted into the yard, ready for distribution to the plastics factory at Brantham during the day.

The signal box, with its 67 levers, was a busy place - and warm, with its coal fire in the corner. Danny Holland, one of the signalmen, remembers his days in the Manningtree box as "the best years of my life". He started at Hackney Downs as a box lad, moving to Mistley in 1971, and then Manningtree in 1972.

In 1980 barriers took the place of the manually worked level crossing gates and the semaphore signalling system was replaced with colour light signalling. This was worked from a new control panel in Manningtree box - the frame and levers having been stripped out.

Four years later a new signalling centre at Colchester took over control from between Marks Tey and Colchester to Ipswich (later to include all signalling to Norwich) thus making several boxes redundant. Danny moved to Colchester in 1985, and the Manningtree signal box was decommissioned, and eventually demolished.

By the level crossing today there is a tall pole with two cameras on the top, which show the signalman at Colchester what is happening on the crossing at any one time. The signalman today can see any road traffic using the crossing before pressing the button which lowers the barriers.

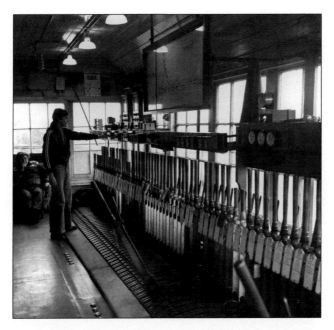

Manningtree Signal Box photographed on 30th September 1978 with Danny Holland (sitting) and Ken Crouch (standing). There were 67 levers in the box.

Danny Holland in the Manningtree signal box in 1980, when the new automatic panel for colour light signalling came into use.

Colchester signalling centre in 1985. The television monitors show the signalmen the level crossings at Ardleigh and Manningtree. The signalling centre takes over signalling from London the Marks Tey side of Colchester.

It was in the spring of 1979 that I made a film record of Manningtree station without commentary, just natural sounds and the men describing their work. The station staff consisted of three senior railmen working a shift pattern throughout the 24 hours.

They were Jim Westwood (he lived in one of the railway cottages close by the level crossing), Colin Churchyard, an ex-signalman, and Mick Turner. Other members of staff included Russell Parker, Paul Osborne, Dick Polley and Harold Barber. Russell and Paul looked after what today are called customer services, and Dick Polley and Harold Barber, who did some of this work, looked after the shunting in the yard and the regular short trips to the plastics factory with trucks of coal and tanks of acid and spirits. For this a small diesel shunting engine arrived from Parkeston to work along to the factory siding in a gap between main line trains. In the early 1980s, just before overhead electrification work began on this line, the siding was closed, and no more shunting was done at Manningtree. Coal for the factory then had to be delivered by road. The factory, making plastics and similar materials, had been on the site since 1887. It closed completely in January 2007.

Other duties by the station staff included cleaning brasses, changing posters in their frames, white lining the platform edges with a special brush that not only did the top, but the side leading down to the line as well, and feeding the goldfish in the small pond that existed on platform 3. This was done away with when new metal fencing was put up at the time of the extensions to the platforms.

Flower beds were lovingly tended to such an extent that the station regularly won Best Kept Station awards. These certificates used to hang in the ticket office, but have disappeared along with coal fires to keep staff and passengers warm, and the framed prints that hung in the waiting rooms of far off railway destinations that you could go to.

The old wooden platform seats had cast iron legs which incorporated the Great Eastern Railway logo, GER. These were replaced with new stylised pressed steel seating in the early 1980s.

The staff room at Manningtree on 30th September 1978. The person on the right is Senior Railman Colin Churchyard.

Inside Manningtree ticket office on 30th September 1978. Note the size of the ticket office window. The old style vertical tickets can be seen in the container on the desk ready to be inserted into the automatic printing machine, which looks like an ordinary till.

Dick Polley giving the signal to the driver that the train is ready to depart. Photographed in July 1979.

The semaphore signals, both in and around the station, and distant signals, were operated mechanically by wire cable from Manningtree signal box. When the signalman operated the lever this pulled the wire that led to the signal. In the event of a broken cable a weight automatically set the signal to danger. This problem did not arise with the points as these were connected to the lever in the signal box by metal rods.

In the box was an illuminated track layout display. The rails were wired in such a way that a light appeared on the display showing where a train was at any one time.

Jim Westwood (on the right) receiving a cheque and thanks after he reported a broken rail at Manningtree.

The semaphore signals were set horizontally for danger. In daylight the red blade of the signal, with a white painted section towards the tip, could be seen a long way away. They had to be, so the drivers could see them from a distance as they came down the incline from Colchester or across the bridges from Ipswich. The signal at the end of platform 2 was a particularly high metal trellis type with a signal at the top and a repeater signal at the bottom for the driver sitting in the station waiting to pull away. A train could only pass if the signal was up.

The system required maintenance, and weekly work for the station staff changing over the oil lamps. Every signal had a paraffin lamp in it to shine through the red or green glass filter attached to the blade, so that if the signal was set at danger, the driver could see the red light at night, or green if he could proceed.

The paraffin lamps would run without refuelling for up to eight days. When low on fuel, the lamps had to be taken out and newly filled lamps put in place. This necessitated a climb up the signal post ladders in all weathers to replace the lamps. The lamps were kept in the lamp room close to the station staff rest room, where they were cleaned, wicks trimmed, and containers filled, ready for the changeover day.

For the more distant signals, such as the one by the Flatford footpath bridge, the staff had to bicycle along the private roadway to the bridge, climb up the bank, and then up the signal ladder to change the paraffin oil lamps.

Dick Polley waving on the diesel shunter and brake van as it descends the slight incline into the goods yard, now the west car park, one day in 1979. The unit travelled twice a day to the plastics factory siding delivering coal and acids and bringing back empty wagons.

The colour light signals, brought into use in 1980, were at first operated from the Manningtree box, then from the signalling centre at Colchester. They have letters before their identification numbers - CO indicating Colchester control. The colour lights are red for danger - the train must stop. Yellow for non stopping trains telling them to slow down as there is a red signal up ahead. Double yellows, that is two yellow lights showing one above another, is in front of a yellow signal, telling the driver that the next signal is yellow, and the following red, so he can be aware that he may have to slow down and stop quite soon.

Where the trains leave the main line for the Harwich branch an angled line of white lights informs the driver he must be ready for the train to go over the points, so he must go slowly. He will already have been warned about this on the previous set of signals he passed by the colour of the light.

Besides the passenger traffic there are a large number of non-stopping trains which include freight trains, ballast trains, maintenance trains, trains of tankers, and specialised trains for spraying lineside weeds. Spent nuclear fuel from Sizewell also passes through the station once a week. Occasionally there is a steam hauled train for railway enthusiasts.

At one time there were long trains of coal and goods trucks trundling along, special wagons for perishables, food in the form of eggs, butter, ham, bacon, and special wagons for cars to and from Harwich, and the train ferry which closed in 1987. This service had opened in 1924 and worked to Zeebrugge.

The Resident Gang

Once there were "lengthmen", who walked the track every day to inspect the rails and crossovers, and a permanent gang at Manningtree. They congregated in the early morning in their hut, (between platform 1 and the approach road) a warm smoky environment, where tea drinking and card playing were part of the relaxation. Their jobs included looking after the fencing on their "patch", as well as any work needed doing on the line, such as checking the gaps between the rail lengths. Before the days of welded rails, the rails came in 60ft or more lengths, held together by a length of metal either side of the join called a "fishplate". There had to be a gap between every length to take account of expansion. After expansion and contraction, and heavy working, the gaps might be out, so part of the gang's responsibilities was to undo the rail length from its tightly held position, and by the use of a wedge and a mallet, drive the length along a bit until the gaps or "breathing switches" as they were known, were the correct width apart to allow for expansion.

The local gang at Manningtree was dispersed in the 1990s, and all maintenance work carried out from central bases at London Road, Ipswich, and their depot at the back of Colchester station. Much of the line work is now not required, as long lengths of welded rail are used which are held very tightly in position. Expansion still occurs, but every so often special overlapping lengths of half rail side by side allow for expansion and contraction. Additional work such as weed control and white lining the edges of the platforms is contracted out to Railscape.

The local gang working on the line between trains in 1979.

Connecting a dropper from the catenary cable to the copper contact wire.

Electrification

The scheme to electrify the main line from London had been envisaged before the 1939 - 1945 war, but it was not until 1949 that the electric cables and their supporting gantries were put in place by BICC (British Insulated Callendar's Cables) between Liverpool Street and Shenfield and an electric train service opened. At that time the overhead supply was 1500 volts DC. Seven years later electrification reached Chelmsford.

The Clacton and Walton-on-Naze branch from Colchester was next wired up in 1959, followed by the gap between Chelmsford and Colchester being completed in 1962. By that time the supply had been changed to 25,000 volts AC, which was considered better from a power transmission efficiency point of view.

Work began in 1984, running into 1985, in and around the Manningtree area on installation of the overhead electricity supply equipment. First came the excavating and concreting train with machines aboard to bore holes by the lineside, then to fill these holes with concrete around a polystyrene "core former". Later the polystyrene middle would be eaten away by the chemical xylene, leaving the concrete base ready with the right size hole in it to receive the steel mast. As two trains were needed to put the steel masts into place, one for the materials and one for the crane, both tracks were necessary, so the work was done on Saturday nights and Sunday mornings. The masts were temporally held upright with wedges, and aligned correctly by a gang working during the day. Next came the grouting train, pouring sand, cement and water into the hole in the space around the mast. After this had set, the wedges were removed. Now the masts were in place.

Then during gaps in traffic the apparatus to hold the overhead cables called cantilever frames were hoisted up onto the masts and bolted into place. Then night working trains came along putting into place the catenary cable followed by the actual copper contact wire hung by droppers from the catenary.

On 18th March 1985, the current was switched on from the Romford control centre. The system, using 25,000 volts AC supplied to the trains, is distributed to the overhead wires from local feeder stations. One of these was built at Manningtree, close to the level crossing.

This all took time, and then it had to be tested, first by gangs with long insulated poles to see that the current was coming through correctly, then by an actual locomotive. The first test runs to Ipswich took place in April 1985, followed by a proper electrified service between Liverpool Street and Ipswich.

Electrification of the line to Norwich was not completed until 1987. The Queen Mother officially opened the electrified line to Norwich at Liverpool Street by naming a reconditioned locomotive Royal Anglian Regiment. Actually the Queen Mother said Royal Anglican Regiment, but nobody seemed to notice.

Manningtree station with freight train July 2007.

2000 Onwards

Going by Bus

During breakdowns, track maintenance, line replacement, and unforeseen incidents, buses are used to transport passengers. A fleet of buses can be called on by the railway to work from station to station - Rail Replacement Buses as they are called.

Perhaps the longest bus replacement time was during the summer of 2004, when Ipswich tunnel was closed for work to enable safer clearance of freight containers. A bus service operated between Manningtree and Ipswich for all passengers from a specially built bus turnaround and car park on the north side of the station. This land, normally the home of sheep and rabbits, was temporally concreted over and a special approach road from the A137 constructed. A stairway was installed up the embankment and over the siding to platform 3, and closed circuit TV cameras installed to monitor passenger movement. Manningtree became "the end of the line" for all London trains. A continuous supply of buses collected and delivered passengers to and from Ipswich. This temporary bus station only had a limited life, for under the special permission required, the land had to revert back to agricultural use. While this was going on the line to Ipswich was re-laid using automatic machines to put down new concrete sleepers and new welded rails.

Manningtree station - west car park July 2007.

The Car Park

The car park has space for 500 cars. The far end, towards Colchester, was the first area to be made into a car park by levelling the goods yard. Here were sidings for wagons, and in the middle stood a goods shed, with rails running through it for loading and unloading goods in the dry. There was also at one time in this yard a weighbridge for trucks and wagons, and a hanging gauge bar – for making sure no truck or wagon was loaded beyond a certain height so that it might strike a bridge. After the goods yard was decommissioned, the shed was let to Sykes Pumps, and the yard used for storing redundant carriages and trucks. It soon fell into a disused state. This area was levelled and made into a car park in the late 1970s. Later, in 1985, the low lying area between the station and the private road, which frequently flooded, was also turned into a car park.

There are plans to increase the size of this car park again. At the time of writing (2007) it costs £5 to leave a car in the car park before 10.00 am. After that the price is £3.50. On Sundays it is only £1.

The inside of the Station Buffet in July 2007. The manageress is Charlotte Sankey, and the cook Katie Johnson.

Station Facilities

The Station Buffet, run by David Wood and Paul Sankey, is a mixture of bar, café, and a place to have lunch. Open all day, until late in the evening, it is a popular venue for passengers and visiting groups with something to celebrate. The manageress is Charlotte Sankey, and the cook Katie Johnson. The owners also run the paper shop, which is open from 5.30 am to 9.00 am.

Station staff are friendly and helpful, particularly when passengers arrive and read the TV announcements stating that there are delays and cancellations.

After the morning rush, Manningtree station settles down to a steady routine. During the day there may be Network Rail people inspecting or carrying out maintenance on the line, or contract staff seeing to the vending machines selling crisps, chocolates and drinks.

The sight on the south viaduct on Saturday 5th May 2007 when a steam special passed through on time at speed on its return journey from London to Dereham. The locomotive is Battle of Britain class locomotive 34067 Tangmere.

On special occasions there may a steam train. On Saturday 5th May 2007 the Norfolkman, a steam special sporting an old name board, passed through on time at speed on its way from Dereham to Liverpool Street. It was pulled by Battle of Britain class locomotive 34067 Tangmere. This steam train special returned through Manningtree at 7.22 in the evening. Many local people and steam enthusiasts lined the platforms, roads and paths close to the line to see this spectacular sight.

One Railway

Today all the passenger trains that run through Manningtree are operated by "One" Railway Company. "One" came into operation on 1st April 2004, following the reorganisation of the franchises in the Anglia area. Before that the passenger trains were run by Anglia Railways and Great Eastern after the demise of British Rail and the setting up of franchises by the Government in 1994.

Passenger traffic has increased enormously over the years, while goods and special loads have decreased. Modern fast-moving freight trains with twenty or more wagons loaded with containers pass regularly through Manningtree. Freight trains are operated by Freightliner and travel between Harwich and the north, Harwich and the south, as well as Felixstowe trains passing through at speed. In the summer of 2007 there was a small increase for a time following the derailment on 22nd June at Ely of part of an EWS (English, Welsh and Scottish Railway) train hauling aggregate wagons to Chelmsford. The line was closed for repairs until the end of 2007. At first freight trains were diverted via Newmarket, but this was reduced after a time and some went the long way round - through Manningtree and via London.

The often congested road layout by Manningtree station. The lorry is queuing to go over the level crossing.

Manningtree station garden July 2007.

Services in 2007

The passenger services to and from London, and Ipswich and beyond, are extensive today compared with only a few years ago. In the 1982 timetable there were only three through trains for the commuters before 9.00 am, then trains throughout the day every two hours.

In 2007 the timetable lists 10 trains to London before 9.00 am, and in the daytime, three per hour - at 18 minutes past the hour (from Norwich), 22 minutes past the hour (from Harwich), and 52 minutes past the hour (from Norwich).

To Ipswich there are two trains per hour which go on to Norwich. There is a through train to Harwich every hour, and the local branch train leaving from platform 1 has two departures in the morning (6.36 and 7.35) and six in the evenings (18.25, 18.57, 19.27, 20.07, 22.38 and 23.38).

The timetable occasionally gets altered if there is severe weather or some form of breakdown. When there are problems all decisions are taken by "control" in London. If there is an overhead line problem, then electricity can be switched off in sections from the overhead power control centre.

The paper and confectionery shop on platform 2. Opening hours 5.30 am to 9.00 am.

Manningtree Station Staff in 2007

Jamie Spurgeon in the ticket office.

David Bramhill helping a passenger get the London train.

Charles Marshall in "the office".

Andy Kerridge waiting for the next train.

David Owers sees off a Harwich train.

Steve Brown sees one of the late commuter trains arrive at Manningtree from London.

There are six staff at Manningtree station working shifts, with additional help when required. Five are known as Hybrid Customer Services staff because of their mixed duties. The mixed duties include train departures, customer service, light cleaning duties, and periodic working in the ticket office.

Then there are the flowers to tend – both tubs and the little flower garden behind the cycle shed. Provided by One Railway these are looked after by David Owers, but the rest of the staff help from time to time.

Other jobs include overriding the automatic station announcer which originates from computer at the control centre in London.

The permanent Manningtree staff are David Bramhill, Steve Brown, Andy Kerridge, Charles Marshall, and David Owers.

The shifts start at 5.15 in the morning with two people on duty until lunchtime. Two come on to relieve them, and they work through to 9.00 pm. At 5.00 pm another railman joins the staff to work through to 11.45 pm. Additional temporary staff appear from time to time as required.

In the ticket Office is Customer Services Supervisor Jamie Spurgeon, who starts work at 5.30 in the morning until relieved at noon. When the ticket office is closed, there is a passenger operated ticket machine which takes cards and cash. If this is not working, then you can get a "permit to travel" by using the machine by the cycle shed.

At 11.45 pm the last railman on duty closes the doors and goes home. There are still a couple of passenger trains from London, the last being the 11.30 from Liverpool Street, which arrives and departs for Norwich at Manningtree at 12.30 am, and passengers have to find their own way out of the station.

It may be the end of another day at this busy, yet rural, station, but throughout the night freight and work trains thunder through. Manningtree station never sleeps.

Manningtree station buffet with teachers 'end of term party' July 2007.

Bibliography

Acworth, W. M., *The Railways of England*, 1900

Allen, Cecil, *Great Eastern*, Ian Allan 1959

Allen, Cecil, *The Great Eastern Railway*, Ian Allan 1968

Cowley, Ian, *Anglia East*, David and Charles 1987

Crump, Norman, *By Rail To Victory - The Story of The LNER in Wartime*, 1947

Glass, Joseph, *Reminiscences of Manningtree and Its Vicinity*, Judd and Glass 1855

Harris, Michael, *The Manningtree to Harwich Branch in The Steam Era*, 2000

Kay, Peter, *Essex Railway Heritage*, Peter Kay 2006

Gordon, D. *A Regional History of The Railways of Great Britain* David and Charles 1968

Hilton, H. F. *The Eastern Union Railway 1846 - 1862*, LNER 1946

Moffat, Hugh, *East Anglia's First Railways*, Terence Dalton 1987

Moult, Margaret, *The Escaped Nun*, Cassell and Company 1909

Norwich Crown Point Open Day, BR 1987

The ABC Railway Guide, 1964, and various published timetables.

Original letters and correspondence of Jim Westwood, Frederick Gant, and Douglas Sheldrake.

Index
Illustrations in bold type